Essential Lives

MOTHER TERESA

MOTHER TERESA

HUMANITARIAN & ADVOCATE FOR THE POOR

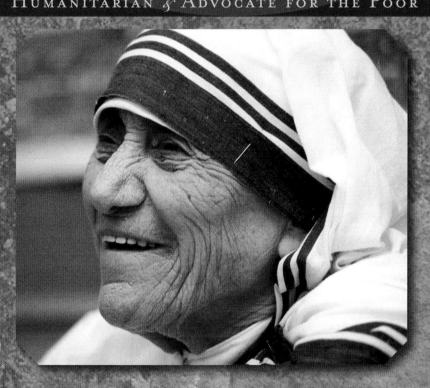

by Christie R. Ritter

Content Consultant:
Kenneth Atkinson
Associate Professor of Religion, University of Northern Iowa

ABDO
Publishing Company

CREDITS

Published by ABDO Publishing Company, 8000 West 78th Street, Edina, Minnesota 55439. Copyright © 2011 by Abdo Consulting Group, Inc. International copyrights reserved in all countries. No part of this book may be reproduced in any form without written permission from the publisher. The Essential Library™ is a trademark and logo of ABDO Publishing Company.

Printed in the United States of America,
North Mankato, Minnesota
112010
012011

 THIS BOOK CONTAINS AT LEAST 10% RECYCLED MATERIALS.

Editor: Amy Van Zee
Copy Editor: Paula Lewis
Interior Design and Production: Kazuko Collins
Cover Design: Kazuko Collins

Library of Congress Cataloging-in-Publication Data
Ritter, Christie R.
  Mother Teresa : humanitarian & advocate for the poor / by Christie R. Ritter.
     p. cm. -- (Essential lives)
  Includes bibliographical references.
  ISBN 978-1-61714-785-2
  1. Teresa, Mother, 1910-1997. 2. Missionaries of Charity--History--20th century. I. Title.
  BX4406.5.Z8R58 2011
  271'.97--dc22
  [B]
                              2010041269

TABLE OF CONTENTS

Agnes Gonxha Bojaxhiu was later known as Mother Teresa and the "Saint of the Gutter" for her work serving the poor.

A LEAP OF FAITH

ister Teresa desperately needed a change of scenery. She was supposed to be on a retreat to relax and leave her responsibilities as a teacher behind for a few weeks. As she rode the train out of the bustling, tropical city of Calcutta,

India, on September 10, 1946, the air grew cooler. The locomotive chugged its way into the mountains toward the resort town of Darjeeling. Finally, she was able to take a deep breath.

The early mornings she usually spent planning lessons and sweeping the classroom floor would give way to quiet, peaceful times of prayer. Sister Teresa would not have to work late into the evenings grading papers. Instead, she could spend those hours studying the Bible or reflecting in quiet contemplation. She could revitalize her spirit by spending a few weeks at the beautiful alpine retreat.

It was there, at the Sisters of Loreto convent in Darjeeling, that she had taken her vows as a nun 15 years earlier. She had promised to serve God for the rest of her life. Becoming a missionary in India had been her childhood dream. Growing up in Europe, India had sounded very exotic. She was enchanted by tales of missionaries living in thatched huts with wild animals roaming nearby. She had eagerly joined the Sisters of Loreto, sailing

Darjeeling

Nestled at the foothills of the Himalayan Mountains, Darjeeling is famous for its tea. Under British rule, it became a popular resort and destination for those escaping the summer heat in the lower elevations of India. It sits at an elevation of 6,710 feet (2,045 m) and is located approximately 300 miles (483 km) from Calcutta. On a clear day, Mount Everest is visible from Darjeeling.

halfway around the world to dedicate her life to doing God's work in India.

Chaos in the Streets

Sister Teresa's work in Calcutta had not brought her into contact with any exotic animals, but there certainly was danger on the streets. The neighborhood outside St. Mary's school and convent where she lived and worked was rarely quiet. The weeks preceding Sister Teresa's retreat had been especially chaotic. In Calcutta, fighting erupted between the Hindu and Muslim populations. Each

Direct Action Day

Hinduism, Buddhism, Jainism, Christianity, Islam, and other religions are all practiced in India. But Hindus and Muslims have had a history of disagreement and violence in the nation, especially during the years leading up to India's independence from Britain in 1947. Britain agreed to grant India independence if a government was set up in the nation. Britain had been dealing mostly with the Indian Congress, which was made up of many Hindus and few Muslims.

The Muslim League, a political party, wanted to make a stand for Muslim independence and wanted their own nation—Pakistan. They wanted their voices to be heard by the British and the Indian Congress. The political party declared Direct Action Day, which fell midway through the Muslim holy month of Ramadan. On Direct Action Day, Muslims burned British buildings. They rioted in the streets, attacking and killing Hindus, who retaliated. Thousands were killed, and many more were left homeless. Eventually, India gained its freedom from Britain and was split into two separate nations: Pakistan and India.

group wanted to control the country. At this time, Muslims made up the majority of the region.

On August 16, 1946, the Muslim League had declared Direct Action Day, which prompted a week of brutal fighting in the streets. Five thousand people died in Calcutta, and three times that number were wounded in the battles around the city. Bodies littered the streets and more than 100,000 people fled the city following the slaughter, fearing the spread of disease.

The rioting meant deliveries of food could not be made to the school. In desperation, Sister Teresa broke the rules of the convent. Nuns were not supposed to leave the safety of the convent, and they were especially forbidden to go into the city alone. But Sister Teresa ventured amidst the battle-torn streets of Calcutta to search for food for the students. When she returned, she had

"People had been jumping over our walls, first a Hindu, then a Muslim. . . . We took in each one and helped him to escape safely. When I went out into the street—only then I saw the death that was following them. A lorry [truck] full of soldiers stopped me and told me I should not be out on the street. . . . I told them I had to come out and take the risk; I had three hundred students who had nothing to eat. The soldiers had rice and they drove me back to the school and unloaded bags of rice."[1]

—Sister Teresa, on Direct Action Day and finding food for her students

An abandoned boy sat injured in the streets of Calcutta after the riots of Direct Action Day.

enough rice to sustain the children for a few more days until the fighting stopped.

A Call within a Call

With the violence of Calcutta fresh in her mind, Sister Teresa gazed out the windows as the train headed higher up into the mountains toward Darjeeling. What happened next turned her world upside down. Sister Teresa never had the retreat she had expected. Instead, in the quiet of those prayerful days, she felt called by God for a different purpose.

God told her she must live among the poorest of the poor. She had spent many years living behind the high walls of St. Mary's school compound, safely protected from the poverty and danger that lay just outside. Now, she felt God wanted her to leave that place of comfort. But would Sister Teresa listen? Could she give up everything she knew and loved, including her friends, her students, and the place she called home? God told her to leave it all behind. She said,

> *The message was quite clear. I was to leave the convent and work with the poor while living among them. It was an order. I knew where I belonged, but I did not know how to get there.* [2]

Rule of Enclosure

The Sisters of Loreto had a rule of enclosure, which meant nuns did not live or work outside the convent. Most of the nuns' interaction with the outside world was with the children who came to the convent's school. The nuns were not allowed to travel freely. When they did go out to seek medical advice or for their annual retreat to the convent in Darjeeling, they traveled in pairs or groups. The rule was intended to help the sisters focus their minds on spiritual matters without distractions from the outside world.

Sacrifice

Leaving St. Mary's school and the Sisters of Loreto was a sacrifice for Sister Teresa. "It was the most difficult thing I have ever done, it was a greater sacrifice than to leave my family and country to enter the religious life," she said.[3]

She knew she could not ignore this call. She felt she had been specially selected for this task. God had spoken to her before, which is what led her to become a nun. But this second message would be more difficult to obey. Sister Teresa knew very little of what life was like outside the convent.

Sister Teresa would have to convince her superiors that the people on the streets of Calcutta needed her more than the students at St. Mary's school did. This harsh new life would put her health and safety at risk. But how could she disobey God's order? Sister Teresa was about to take a leap of faith.

Mother Teresa in 1979

Skopje, where Mother Teresa lived as a child

GROWING UP

S ister Teresa was not born into poverty.

Her family led a comfortable life, and by all accounts, she was a happy child. She was born on August 26, 1910, and christened the following day with the name Agnes Gonxha Bojaxhiu. Her parents,

Nikola and Dranafile (Drana) Bojaxhiu were Albanian by ethnic origin, but the family lived in the town of Skopje in what was then part of the Ottoman Empire. It is in the southeastern part of Europe on the Balkan Peninsula between Italy and Greece.

Agnes was the youngest child in her family. Her brother, Lazar, was three years older, and her sister, Aga, was six years older. The Bojaxhius had been Catholics for many generations. However, most people who lived in the area were not. At the center of the Roman Catholic Church is the teaching that Jesus Christ is the son of God and that he came to Earth in the form of man. He was born of the Virgin Mary. He performed miracles, had followers called apostles, and died nailed on a cross for the sins of the world to be forgiven. On the third day after his death, he rose from the dead and ascended into heaven. Catholics pray to Jesus, believing he is a spiritual force in their everyday lives.

Catholics believe God chose Mary, who was pure, to be the mother of Jesus. He was conceived by God

Flower Bud

Gonxha, an Albanian name that translates to "flower bud" in English, was Agnes's middle name. It was also a nickname the family called her. As the youngest, she was a little flower bud and remembered as a happy, obedient little girl who did well in school and was a devout Catholic from a young age.

placing Jesus in her womb. Catholics believe Mary is holy in her own right.

The Bojaxhiu family attended the nearby Church of the Sacred Heart, a Roman Catholic church that played a central role in their educational and spiritual lives. Being part of both the Albanian and Catholic minority in Skopje, the Bojaxhius held tightly to their cultural origins. Actively participating in the church helped them to do so. Drana made sure her children prayed together daily.

Skopje and the Balkans

Archeologists believe people have lived in the area around Skopje for at least 25 centuries. Today, this region is known as the Balkan Peninsula. Rulers and tribes have long waged war over the area, which is a vital crossroads for trade in Europe.

While the city was under the rule of the Roman Empire, Skopje was known as Scupi. After the fourth century CE, Scupi was a center of Christianity. When the Christian church split into the Eastern Orthodox and Roman Catholic divisions, most of the countries in the Balkans followed the Orthodox tradition. Slavic tribes from the north settled in the Balkans in the sixth century.

By the fourteenth century, Turkish invaders controlled much of Europe, including the Balkans, under their Ottoman Empire. They brought with them the religion of Islam and named the town Uskub. By the late nineteenth century, the Ottoman Empire had lost Bulgaria, Serbia, and much of the Balkans that it had occupied for centuries. Muslims fled those areas and many settled in Skopje, which remained under Ottoman rule. As a result, Christians, especially Catholics, became a minority among Muslims in the region. In 1913, Skopje officially became part of Serbia, and later Yugoslavia. Today, Skopje is a city of approximately 500,000 people. It is the capital of Macedonia, which became an independent republic in 1991.

In 1919, Agnes's father died. He had been a successful businessman, merchant, and builder. After his death, life for the family became difficult. It was up to Drana to provide for the family. After a time of mourning, Drana began a business of sewing and embroidering cloth. Although they were never wealthy, she managed to keep her children fed.

Drana made sure the children understood that having material things in life was not nearly as important as being a person of good character. She taught them by example. Often, Drana would invite those who were less fortunate to share a meal with her family. Many times, she helped neighbors in need by cleaning their homes or running errands. Her children learned that sharing what they had, whether it was food, clothing, or time, was a routine part of life.

A Talented Father

Nikola Bojaxhiu was a busy man of many interests and talents. A member of Skopje's town council, he ran several successful businesses in partnership with some of the town's other leading citizens. He traveled all over the Balkans buying and selling merchandise. He spoke five languages: Albanian, French, Serbo-Croat, Italian, and Turkish.

Bojaxhiu wanted to see an independent nation of Albania, and this controversial viewpoint may have been what led to his death at age 45. He had traveled to a political gathering in Belgrade, Yugoslavia, to advocate for Albanian independence. When he returned to Skopje, he was very ill and soon died. His family and doctors believed political enemies had poisoned him.

CALLED TO SERVE

During the earliest years of their education, the Bojaxhiu children attended the Sacred Heart Church school and were taught in the Albanian language. Agnes and Aga sang in the church choir and belonged to the Sodality of Children of Mary, a group for young Catholic girls. Later they attended state-run schools where lessons were held in the Serbo-Croatian language. From a very young age, Agnes showed unquestioning acceptance of authority. Her brother, Lazar, recalled that she admonished him for complaining about a strict priest, Father Zadrima, who was very unpopular with the young people. Agnes told her brother it was his duty to respect Christ's priest.

Agnes first learned about the work of Catholic missionaries from Father Franjo Jambreković. He was a young Jesuit priest who came to

An Early Calling

The Bojaxhiu family made an annual pilgrimage to the shrine of Our Lady of Cernagore. The shrine is located in the hill town of Letnice, Montenegro, outside Skopje. As a child, Agnes had been ill with malaria and whooping cough. Her mother thought the mountain air might benefit her youngest daughter's health. Families traveled in horse-drawn carriages up to the shrine. There, they prayed in the chapel dedicated to Mary, the mother of Jesus Christ. Mother Teresa said it was at this chapel where, at age 12, she first felt God calling her to become a missionary.

Skopje in 1925. He shared stories with his youth group members about his fellow Jesuit priests, who had been missionaries in India.

Agnes recalled that she felt God first spoke to her at age 12, while she prayed at a shrine outside Skopje. When she was 18, she turned to Father Jambreković to help her decide whether she should answer God's call and dedicate her life to becoming a missionary. She was drawn to the religious life, but she was not sure if she was ready to take the major step of entering a convent to become a Catholic nun. She later said her mother's advice stayed with her long after her decision was made. "She often repeated to me, 'When you accept a task, do it willingly. If not, don't accept it.'"[1] For young Agnes, the decision of how she was to spend her life was not hers, but one she put in God's hands. Many years later, she recalled while gesturing to heaven, "He made the choice."[2]

Memorial in Skopje

The Memorial House of Mother Teresa is built on the site of the church she attended as a child in Skopje. At the site, people can learn more about what life was like in Skopje when Mother Teresa was growing up there. Exhibits include photographs and personal items that once belonged to Mother Teresa.

The news of her daughter's decision came as a shock to Drana, even though she had always urged her children to devote themselves to God. Upon hearing the news that Agnes had decided to become a nun, Drana isolated herself in her room for 24 hours. She was likely praying that God would allow her to overcome her grief at giving up her daughter for a life of service and give her an acceptance that this would be a fulfillment of God's calling to Agnes. When Drana came out, she had accepted the decision, but she must have known that her beloved child's life would never be the same. With her mother's blessing, Agnes was now free to follow her dream. A large group of friends came to the train station to bid farewell to Agnes. Drana and Aga traveled with Agnes from Skopje to Zagreb, Yugoslavia. It was the first part of a long journey to the place where Agnes would go for training—and it was the last time Agnes would ever see her mother and sister.

At a young age, Mother Teresa felt called to serve God as a missionary.

Nuns entered the chapel at one of Mother Teresa's Missionaries of Charity convents in 1996.

ENTERING RELIGIOUS LIFE

gnes knew that making the decision to become a Catholic nun was very serious. Nuns promise to live lives of chastity, obedience, and poverty. This means not only devoting oneself to a life of service to God, but also the separation from one's family and a promise to never marry and have children. It also includes the possibility of being sent to faraway, unfamiliar, and dangerous lands. Agnes was aware of these sacrifices when she left her home and family in Skopje to begin her new life.

Agnes had learned through the Jesuit priests that there was a group of nuns working in India. This group, called an order, was named the Sisters of Loreto. Agnes decided to join them. On September 26, 1928, Agnes said good-bye to her mother and sister in Zagreb, Yugoslavia, where she was joined by a girl named Betika. The two young women traveled together by train to Paris, France, where they were interviewed by a Loreto sister to determine if they would be suitable candidates for the missionary work in India. They passed that initial interview and continued their

Church Hierarchy

The Roman Catholic Church is based in Rome, Italy, at the Vatican. The Vatican is an independent city-state, which has its own laws and government. The church has a hierarchy with a leader who is called the pope. Below the pope is the College of Cardinals, many of whom are bishops who serve local churches. Upon the death of the pope, the College of Cardinals is responsible for electing a new pope, who serves for the rest of his life. Each region of the world is governed by a Catholic diocese. Many large cities have their own dioceses, which oversee parishes (also called churches), schools, hospitals, and other services.

Agnes lived near Dublin during her time in Ireland.

travels to Ireland, to a Sisters of Loreto house at
Rathfarnham, near Dublin. Agnes and Betika
stayed there for six weeks studying English, which
was completely new to them. English was to become
Agnes's primary language for the rest of her life.

In 1928, Catholic women interested in becoming
nuns began their training as postulants. A postulancy
is a trial period of time to explore what life is like as
a nun before making any long-term commitment
to the Roman Catholic Church. The trial period
may last from several weeks up to two years. It gives

the religious order, in this case, the Sisters of Loreto, time to get to know the postulant and determine whether she is well suited for life as a nun.

A postulant wears a long, white dress, called a habit, and a black veil, which covers the top of her head, but not her face. In keeping with Catholic tradition, Agnes chose a new name during her postulancy in Ireland. The selection of a new name, usually the name of a saint, acknowledges that the postulant is leaving behind her old life and starting a new life with God. At Rathfarnham, Agnes chose the name Mary Teresa of the Child Jesus. She was called Sister Teresa for short. Her friend from Yugoslavia, Betika, chose the name Sister Mary Magdalene.

Although she spent only six weeks in Ireland, Agnes, now Sister Teresa, was ready for what lay ahead. She had completed her training as a postulant and gained a basic understanding

Loreto Abbey

In lush and green Ireland, Agnes and Betika found a place very different from their homes in the Balkans. Located at the foothills of the Dublin Mountains, Loreto Abbey is one of several large and stately Georgian-style buildings at Rathfarnham. Georgian-style buildings are characterized by their symmetrical style with centered doors and rectangular windows. Buildings were typically made of brick or stone. The style was popular from the eighteenth century until the early nineteenth century and is named after England's Kings George I, II, III, and IV.

Construction of Loreto Abbey began in 1725. Later, a church, a concert hall, and school buildings were added. Soon, it was regarded as one of the best schools for girls in Ireland. Loreto Abbey became the headquarters of 22 Sisters of Loreto convents around the world. The order began sending missionaries to India from Ireland in 1841.

of English. She also belonged to an order of nuns with a strong presence in India and a long history of service to the needy. After her postulancy, Sister Teresa would pass through a novice period. But Sister Teresa would not spend her time as a novice in Ireland. Instead, she would travel to the very place she had dreamed of as a child. On December 1, 1928, she and the other novices set sail for a new life.

Sister Teresa sailed on the *Marcha* to India by way of the Suez Canal. The ship traveled through the Red Sea and south into the Indian Ocean before reaching the Bay of Bengal. The group celebrated Christmas on the ship. Sister Teresa was disappointed that a Catholic priest was not present to hold a Mass service for the sacred holiday. She debarked in Colombo, Ceylon (now Sri Lanka), for a short time. Afterward, a Catholic priest joined the group, and

Namesake

Agnes chose the name Teresa in honor of Saint Thérèse of Lisieux, a French nun and patron saint of missions. Saint Thérèse was born in 1873 and died at age 24 from tuberculosis. She never performed any great deeds, but she continually made small sacrifices, such as smiling at those she did not like or taking the blame for things she did not do. She was never a missionary, but she prayed and wrote letters of support for the missions. She encouraged others to find God in ordinary events.

they were able to have a daily Mass, which was a great comfort to Sister Teresa.

She must have been shocked by the poverty of the people she saw on her first port of call in India. She wrote a letter that appeared in the November 1931 issue of *Catholic Mission* magazine. In it, she described the sights in Madras, India:

Many families live in the streets, along the city walls, even in places thronged with people. Day and night they live out in the open. . . . As we went along the street we chanced upon one family gathered around a dead relation, wrapped in worn red rags, strewn with yellow flowers, his face painted in colored stripes. . . . If our people could only

Mary Ward

The Sisters of Loreto is the common name of a group of Catholic nuns formally known as the Institute of the Blessed Virgin Mary. English-woman Mary Ward founded the group in 1609. During her life, the Roman Catholic Church was under attack in England so she went to France in pursuit of religious freedom. She had a radical idea at the time to form a religious group that would be governed by women who would not be confined to a convent. She and her followers provided spiritual care, tended to the poor and the sick, and started schools in France, Belgium, Austria, and Germany. The church did not approve of her woman-led society and had her imprisoned.

Considered a pioneer in the Roman Catholic Church, Mary Ward forged a new path that continues today. The Sisters of Loreto continue the work of their founder by caring for the poor and the ill, teaching and counseling, and serving as missionaries around the world.

The Lives of Nuns and Priests

Priests also undergo training similar to nuns in preparation for their life-long commitment to the Roman Catholic Church. Priests and nuns often work together. The rules of the church do not permit women to become priests. Nuns are not permitted to say Mass, perform weddings and baptisms, or listen to confessions.

see all this, they would stop grumbling about their own misfortunes and offer thanks to God for blessing them with such abundance.[1]

New ways of life surrounded the young woman—she saw curious and strange sights. It would not be long before Sister Teresa would set foot in a place with which she would forever be associated: Calcutta, India.

A street beggar in Madras, India, circa 1930

Chapter

4

The Himalayas can be viewed from the town of Darjeeling.

EARLY YEARS AS A NUN

ister Teresa arrived at her final destination of Calcutta, India, on January 6, 1929. She wrote,

> *With a joy which I cannot describe, we touched the soil of Bengal for the first time. In the convent church we first of*

all offered up our thanks to the Redeemer for allowing us to arrive safely at our destination.[1]

Calcutta was to be her home for the rest of her life, but her first stay was brief. After only a week, she was sent to the mountain town of Darjeeling, where the Sisters of Loreto had a convent. She spent the next two years in the convent as a novice.

After completing a postulancy, nuns-in-training such as Sisters Teresa and Mary Magdalene spend the next two years as novices. During this part of their training, novices often serve as teachers or nurses and deepen their relationship with God through prayer and study of the Scriptures. After two years as a novice, if the sister decides the religious life is the right vocation for her, she makes her first temporary vows. Taking these vows means she is making a commitment for six to nine years of service.

During this time, nuns are expected to mature further in their spiritual lives and continue their

Christians in India

The earliest Christian in India was one of Jesus Christ's 12 apostles, Thomas, who arrived in the year 52 CE. Portuguese missionaries introduced Catholic teachings in the sixteenth century. Protestant churches came to India beginning in the eighteenth century. Christian missionaries built schools and churches and converted many Indians to Christianity. This was not always welcomed by the Hindu and Muslim Indians.

work of service to the church and community. After this period, permanent vows are taken, meaning they have chosen to make a lifelong commitment to devote their lives to serving Jesus Christ.

Some orders, but not Sister Teresa's order, follow the tradition of being cloistered, which means they do not have interaction with the outside world. They spend their lives inside a convent and do work for the church, such as sewing clothing for nuns and priests, making the wafers used in communion during Mass, or other tasks needed for the church operations.

During her novitiate, Sister Teresa continued her studies of English but also learned

Darjeeling Clinic

Many of the people who came to the clinic in Darjeeling walked for hours to get there. The clinic offered the only medical care available to some of them, and the nuns were known to have skills and medicines. But sometimes the cases were so desperate that all the nuns could offer was compassion and prayer. In one such case, Sister Teresa wrote,

Finally a man arrives with a bundle from which two dry twigs protrude. They are the legs of a child. The little boy is very weak. I realize he is near to death and hurry to bring him holy water. The man is afraid that we do not want to take the child, and says, "If you do not want him, I will throw him into the grass. The jackals will not turn up their noses at him." My heart freezes. The poor child! Weak, and blind—totally blind. With much pity and love I take the little one into my arms, and fold him in my apron. The child has found a second mother.[2]

the languages of the people in India: Bengali and Hindu. She began teaching local students in Darjeeling and was assigned to work in a medical clinic. There, she vividly saw more of the widespread poverty and sickness in India. On May 24, 1931, in Darjeeling, Sister Teresa finished her novitiate and took her first temporary vows as a nun. She was 20 years old.

St. Mary's School

Sister Teresa left the quiet mountain refuge of Darjeeling and entered the new life the Sisters of Loreto had chosen for her: teaching in the hot, humid, bustling city of Calcutta. St. Mary's school was part of the Sisters of Loreto's campus in the neighborhood of Entally. The campus buildings included classrooms, a convent where the nuns lived, and buildings housing the orphanage. High walls separated the campus from the poverty around it.

The children who attended the schools came from many different backgrounds. Some were children of the wealthy British colonialists who controlled India at the time. These colonialists could afford to send their children to a good school. Other children were from middle-class Indian families.

A Spiritual Adviser

Sister Teresa often sought the counsel of priests when she was faced with a difficult choice. Father Julien Henry was a priest and a spiritual adviser to Mother Teresa from her earliest days in India and had witnessed her growing concern for the poor. He said, "She felt an inner prompting to do something to relieve the hardships of the very poor, and to lead them to God. Spiritually they were completely neglected—truly sheep without a shepherd. She realized that within the structures of organized education, aimed mainly at the middle classes, in which she worked, it would be impossible to achieve this aim. She had to get out of the system and start something quite different."[3]

Still others were orphans who were taken in and educated for free.

Having mastered both English and the local Bengali language, Sister Teresa taught history, and later geography, to many of the poorest children at St. Teresa's, a nearby school. She was well liked by her students and highly regarded by the other nuns, who took to calling her "Bengali Teresa" to distinguish her from another Loreto nun who had also chosen the name Teresa. Eventually, Sister Teresa was made principal of the School of St. Teresa and director of the Daughters of St. Anne, another order that ran the school.

Life in Calcutta

The Sisters of Loreto nuns did not often go outside the convent. However, by 1935, Sister Teresa's additional teaching job at St. Teresa's required that she leave the convent and walk out into the streets of Calcutta to reach the school. This experience further opened her eyes to the wretched lives of those around her. Her future path was laid by each step she took along the way and each interaction she had with the poor. She said,

> *When I first saw where the children slept and ate, I was full of anguish. It is not possible to find worse poverty. And yet, they are happy. Blessed childhood! Though when we first met, they were not at all joyful. They began to leap and sing only when I had put my hand on each dirty little head. From that day onwards they called me "Ma," which means "Mother."*[4]

Having completed six years since making her temporary vows, she was now ready to make her lifelong commitment to serving Jesus Christ. In May 1937, Sister Teresa took her final vows at the convent in

A Gentle Reminder

After taking her final vows, Mother Teresa wrote a letter to her mother telling her that she loved her work and that she now headed a whole school. Her mother's response was a reminder and possibly a wake-up call. "Dear child, do not forget that you went to India for the sake of the poor," Drana wrote, reminding her of a poor woman they used to care for in Skopje named Filé. "She was covered in sores, but what made her suffer much more was the knowledge that she was alone in the world . . . that she had been forgotten by her family."[5]

Darjeeling. She was made headmistress of St. Mary's school when she returned to Calcutta. From that time on, she was known as Mother Teresa.

In the 1930s, India was a place of religious diversity. Indians celebrated Christmas with a fair in Calcutta in 1933.

Police attempted to restore order after a political demonstration in Delhi in 1942.

TROUBLES IN INDIA

t the beginning of the twentieth
century, Britain was the most powerful
nation in the world. Its colonies stretched around
the globe, which made it very wealthy. Since 1858,
Britain had ruled India. As a colony, India had

participated in World War I by sending money and 800,000 troops to support Britain.

India had hoped to be rewarded for its loyalty to the British Crown by being given more independence. But that was not the case, and very few Indians held jobs of importance in government or had the power to vote in their own country. After World War I, there was a growing resentment of the British rulers. Many Indians joined in a movement for self-government. Sister Teresa came to India during the time of British rule when British government officials lived in elegant homes while many Indians starved in the streets. During the years she taught at Loreto Entally, from 1931 to 1948, there were protests, marches, and violence as India fought its way to independence. In 1947, the British divided British India into two separate and independent nations: India and Pakistan.

Gandhi and Nehru

The Indian National Congress was created in 1885 to give educated Indians a voice in their own nation's government. Over the following decades, it became the main organization advocating for independence from Britain. Two of its leaders were Mahatma Gandhi and Jawaharlal Nehru. Gandhi became famous for his campaigns aimed at gaining freedom and civil rights for Indians. Nehru went on to become the first prime minister of the nation of India.

Finding Her Place

Sister Teresa had sacrificed all that was important to her—her family, her homeland, her friends—and chosen to dedicate herself to becoming a missionary in India, where she felt she was most needed. But in her role as a teacher in a school that was populated by many of the children of the wealthy, she may have felt that her sacrifice was wasted. The privileged upper- and middle-class families who could afford to send their children to the school were not those who needed her. It was the poor whom she had come to help.

One of the most difficult periods for Indians came toward the end of World War II. The war had begun in 1939 in Europe with the advance of

Gandhi's Salt March

Mahatma Gandhi grabbed the attention of the world when he embarked on his Salt March of 1930. He undertook this nonviolent protest and act of civil disobedience to point out the unfairness of a tax the British had placed on salt. Salt is required by the human body, but the tax made salt very expensive for poor Indians to buy. They were forbidden from harvesting salt from the sea or from selling it. This gave the British a monopoly on its sale and production.

Gandhi walked 240 miles (386.2 km) in 23 days, gathering followers and speaking to people in every town along the way. On the last day, he came to the ocean, where he broke the law by picking up a lump of salt. He was later arrested and jailed along with many of his followers. But by engaging in a nonviolent protest, he had won a symbolic victory for the cause of Indian independence from Britain and launched the modern civil disobedience movement.

the German Nazis into Poland, Austria, France, and other countries. In 1941, Japan brought the United States into the war by bombing the US Naval Fleet at Pearl Harbor in Hawaii. This led to a war on two fronts: Europe in the west and Asia in the east. The Japanese invaded India in 1944. The Japanese were defeated in 1945, but the havoc created by the war led to the deaths of more than 1 million Indians, many by starvation.

It was against this backdrop that Mother Teresa received her second call from God while riding the train to Darjeeling on September 10, 1946. She had witnessed the bloody riots in the streets of Calcutta when she had gone outside the convent to get food for her students.

A New Path

This second call from God set Mother Teresa on a new path, but there were many hurdles she had to

Religious Divisions in India and Partition

After World War II, Britain changed its focus from maintaining its empire to rebuilding its homeland. As a result, India finally won its independence from Britain on August 15, 1947. Peace did not rule the newly formed nations of India and Pakistan. The end of British India brought about a massive redistribution of the population based on religion. In the months after partition, much of the Hindu population left Pakistan and many Muslims left India. People feared what might happen to them as a minority if they stayed in a land ruled by the majority. This division of India was the largest migration in human history. Between 10 and 15 million people uprooted from what had been their homelands. Fighting among the fleeing refugees left an estimated 1 million people dead.

A Healthy Diet

When Mother Teresa first began her ministry to the poor, she planned to eat the way the poor did. This consisted of a diet of only rice and salt. Mother Dengal was the head of the Medical Mission Sisters in Patna where Mother Teresa had gone for medical training. Mother Dengal discouraged Mother Teresa from this plan. Mother Dengal said such a diet would not keep her healthy and, without proper nutrition, she would probably become ill with the same kind of diseases that sickened and killed those she was trying to help. Mother Teresa took the advice and added fruits, legumes, vegetables, and other nutritious foods to her diet.

overcome before she could begin her ministry to the poorest of the poor in Calcutta. She needed approval from the Roman Catholic officials who oversaw her work as a Sister of Loreto. Upon her return to Calcutta, she explained to Father Celeste Van Exem that God told her she must help the poor. He later recalled that he believed Mother Teresa's calling was genuine because she was such an ordinary person: "Mother was not an exceptional person. She was an ordinary Loreto nun, a very ordinary person but with great love for her Lord."[1]

The news of Mother Teresa's request came as a surprise to her fellow nuns and priests. In 1946, her idea was radical: a European nun, free from the rules of the convent, able to walk among the people of the Calcutta slums. The approval process took two years and required the approval of the Vatican. Finally,

Mother Teresa had the blessing she sought from the pope to work outside the convent and help the poor. When she left Loreto Entally in August 1948, she was the first Catholic nun in 300 years to be allowed to work outside a convent.

She would no longer be a Sister of Loreto, but she had the blessing of the order to pursue her work with the poor. The general superior of the Loreto Order at Rathfarnham in Ireland wrote to Mother Teresa, telling her:

> If this is the will of God, then I give you permission with all my heart. You can count on the friendship and esteem of all of us here. And if for any reason you want to come back here, we shall accept you again gladly as our Sister. [2]

Mother Teresa traded her nun's habit for a sari, the traditional clothing of Indian women. The cloth is often wrapped around a woman's waist and over one shoulder. Although some are made of expensive silk, Mother Teresa purchased hers at a market. It was the simplest and cheapest she could find. She wore rough leather sandals. Pinned to her left shoulder was a crucifix. To prepare her for working with the sick people of the slums, she was sent for training to another order, the Medical Mission Sisters, at a

hospital in Patna, approximately 350 miles
(563 km) from Calcutta. She spent several weeks
learning the nursing skills she would need for the
job that lay ahead. ⌐

Mother Teresa's sari was shown in an exhibit in Rome, Italy, in 2003.

Mother Teresa in November 1960

Ministry to the Poor

other Teresa had been in India for nearly 20 years, faithfully and happily teaching at the Loreto schools. So, on the first day of her ministry to the poor in Calcutta, she did what came naturally. She began teaching children who could not afford to go to school. She rented a hut in the slum called Motijhil with five Indian rupees that she had been given when she left the Sisters of Loreto. She had no pencils, books, or desks. She taught her first lessons by scratching the Bengali alphabet in the dirt with a stick. People began to give furniture and books for her school. She soon gained more students. In addition, three other teachers volunteered to help her.

Mother Teresa knew the families in the slums needed more than education. Her work expanded to include caring for the sick and the hungry. She sent "begging letters" to those she thought might donate. Donations of money came in from Hindus and Muslims, and she was able to open a dispensary to give medicine to the sick.

From the very first days of her ministry to the poor, she demonstrated the incredible determination that would make her well known first in Calcutta, then around the world. One day, she made a list of medicines she needed and

Muslim Minority

Muslims were a minority in India when it was under British rule. The Muslim League was active in the Indian independence movement and backed the idea of a separate homeland for Muslims, which eventually came to be Pakistan. In Pakistan, Muslims made up the majority of the population; a small number of Hindus stayed in the area.

showed it to a pharmacist in his shop. He told her he could not help her. Instead of leaving, she sat down and prayed her rosary. At the end of the day, she was still there praying. The pharmacist, who could see what he was up against, gathered up all the medicines Mother Teresa had asked for and gave them to her free of charge.

BEGINNING THE MISSIONARIES OF CHARITY

The first nuns to join Mother Teresa were her former students—all Bengali girls. The first was Subhasini Das, who took the name Sister Agnes in honor of Mother Teresa's birth name. As more nuns joined, it became time for Mother Teresa to formalize her group into a new congregation with its own rules and constitution. She called this new order the Missionaries of Charity. Nuns who joined her agreed to the three traditional vows: chastity, obedience, and poverty. In addition, they pledged a fourth vow: wholehearted and free service to the poorest of the poor. They would live like the poor and own only three saris, a pair of sandals, a bucket for cleaning, and their Bibles. They would not take money from the government, but only from people who wanted to give freely.

The young women who wanted to join Mother Teresa had to possess certain qualities to do the difficult work they would be asked to do for the rest of their lives. She required that they be of healthy mind and body, able to learn, possess common sense, and have a cheerful disposition. They would begin by familiarizing themselves with the work for six months. Then, if they wanted to continue, they would become postulants for a year. After that initial training, they would take their first vows, which would be

Constitution of the Society of the Missionaries of Charity

On October 7, 1950, the Constitution of the Society of the Missionaries of Charity was approved by the papacy in Rome. It reads:

Our object is to quench the thirst of Jesus Christ on the cross by dedicating ourselves freely to serve the poorest of the poor, according to the work and teaching of Our Lord, thus announcing the Kingdom of God in a special way.

Our special mission is to work for the salvation and holiness of the poorest of the poor. As Jesus was sent by the Father, so he sends us, full of his spirit, to proclaim the gospel of his love and pity among the poorest of the poor throughout the world.

Our special task will be to proclaim Jesus Christ to all peoples, above all to those who are in our care. We call ourselves Missionaries of Charity.

"God is love." The missionary must be a missionary of love, must always be full of love in his soul and must also spread it to the souls of others, whether Christian or not.[1]

renewed each year for six years, before taking the final vows. Mother Teresa said,

> This is the only way we will be in a position to share the sufferings of the poor. Strict poverty is our only safeguard. We do not want to happen to us what happened to other religious orders . . . that started out serving the poor and . . . ended up serving the rich.[2]

She believed that God guided her work. She did not worry about where the money would come from to support her charity and said,

> I never give it a thought. It always comes. We do all our work for our Lord. He must look after us. If He wants something done, He must provide us with the means. If He does not provide us with the means, then it shows that He does not want that particular work. I forget about it.[3]

Mother Teresa and the sisters in the Missionaries of Charity started out in a room of a home owned by a Catholic family, but they soon outgrew that space. A Muslim man who had heard of Mother Teresa's charitable works sold his house to the Archdiocese of Calcutta, to be used by Mother Teresa, for far less than what it was worth. He was happy that it would bring a benefit to the community. "God gave me this house," he said. "I give it back to Him."[4] After

Mother Teresa took it over, the house became known as the Mother House, the headquarters of the Missionaries of Charity.

Ministry to the Dying

The work the nuns did was often unpleasant and difficult. The schedule they kept was grueling. On a typical day, the sisters rose before 5:00 a.m. to go to Mass and pray. Afterward, they had breakfast and did chores before going out into the city in pairs to help the poor and sick. They either walked where they were going or took public transportation. When they were working, they were not permitted to accept anything, including food and drink. This rule, according to Mother Teresa, was so that the poor did not give away things in gratitude that they could not afford to go without. The nuns returned to the Mother House for lunch and a rest before going out to work again until 6:00 p.m. They had dinner together and a bit of time to relax before evening prayers. Bedtime was 10:00 p.m.

"I never look at the masses as my responsibility. I look only at the individual. I can love only one person at a time. I can feed only one person at a time. Just one, one, one. You get closer to Christ by coming closer to each other. As Jesus said, 'Whatever you do to the least of my brethren, you do it to me.' So you begin . . . I begin. I picked up one person—maybe if I didn't pick up that one person I wouldn't have picked up the others."[5]

—Mother Teresa

Going out into the slums every day, Mother Teresa could see that people who needed her help were all around. She began picking up sick people off the streets of Calcutta, putting them in wheelbarrows, and taking them to hospitals. Once there, she pleaded with the already overwhelmed doctors and nurses to take in and treat just one more person. Sometimes her request was denied, and she was told the person would die soon anyway. Workers at the hospital said they needed to save the hospital beds for people who had a chance of getting better. Mother Teresa refused to accept this. In one case, she refused to take a dying woman back to the street.

"In the end, because I insisted, they took her in," she said. The hospital put a mattress on the floor for the woman, who died a few hours later. "It was then that I decided to find a place for the dying and take care of them myself."[6]

Mother Teresa wanted to give comfort and care to the dying in their final days. To help her, local authorities offered her the use of a building that was next to a Hindu

"I think it was worth while having that [Home for the Dying Destitutes] even for those few people to die beautifully, with God and in peace."[7]

—*Mother Teresa*

The nuns at Nirmal Hriday have been caring for patients
for more than half a century.

shrine called the Kali Temple. It was here that
Hindus came for religious ceremonies and to pray
to the goddess Kali. In 1952, the building became
Mother Teresa's Home for the Dying Destitutes,
or Nirmal Hriday, which means "Place of the
Immaculate Heart."

Mother Teresa was able to bring people she had
found on the streets of Calcutta to her refuge for the

Leprosy

Leprosy is an infectious disease that was rampant in the streets of Calcutta when Mother Teresa began her ministry. The disease causes sores on the skin, numbness and swelling of the arms and legs, and can lead to deformity and blindness.

People were fearful of catching the leprosy bacteria from others, which is spread by droplets from the nose and mouth. Lepers were sometimes sent to live in leper colonies. Infected people were often shunned by their families and left to fend for themselves. If caught early, leprosy can be cured completely by medicine.

Mother Teresa came up with the idea of a mobile clinic, which would bring medical care to the lepers. This would save those who were infected, who often had sores on their feet, from walking long distances to receive care.

dying. She told a story about a man lying in the gutter of the street. His entire body was covered in wounds except for his face. He was very sick and near death when she found him. She took him in. "I have lived like an animal in the street, but I am going to die like an angel, loved and cared for," he told her.[8] After three hours, he died with a smile on his face.

At first, some Indian people were not happy that a Catholic woman was taking care of people so close to a sacred Hindu temple. They worried that she was there to convert Indians to Christianity. Some people threw stones at the sisters of the Missionaries of Charity as they brought the dying people in from the streets. Mother Teresa received death threats. Her reply was, "If you kill us, we would only hope to reach God sooner."[9]

Mother Teresa invited the city leaders to go inside Nirmal Hriday to see the work the sisters were doing. The leaders saw how the nuns applied medicine to the wounds and cleaned the filth and excrement off the bodies of the lepers. They saw how the sisters patiently fed those who were too weak to feed themselves. After viewing this, a police official went outside and told the crowd of protesters,

> *Yes, I will send this woman away, but only after you have persuaded your mothers and sisters to come here to do the work that she is doing. This woman is a saint.*[10]

However, not everyone agreed. One person who worked with Mother Teresa in the early days became a harsh critic. Dr. Marcus Fernandes agreed to oversee the medical care at Nirmal Hriday when he could spare the time away from his duties at the hospital. He saw that the care was haphazard and did not follow traditional medical practices. Many patients did not have life-threatening illnesses, but treatable problems such as malnutrition. He made suggestions to Mother Teresa about how to improve the care but said she would not listen. He became very discouraged after several years, especially when donations were pouring in, but patient outcomes did not improve.

Prince Charles visited Mother Teresa's Shishu Bhavan in 1980.

Caring for the Children

After establishing her Home for the Dying
Destitutes, Mother Teresa turned her focus to the
needs of children. At that time in Calcutta, there
were many children whose parents had died from
starvation, leprosy, tuberculosis, or another of the
many diseases that were rampant in India. Many
children were left with no one to take care of them.
Some were sick and needed medical attention.
Others had been abandoned on the streets by parents
who could not afford to feed them.

In 1955, Mother Teresa opened a home for children called Shishu Bhavan. Word spread throughout Calcutta that hospitals, social workers, or anyone needing to find a home for a child could bring the child to Mother Teresa. She would not turn away any child from the doors of her children's home. Shishu Bhavan became a last refuge and quickly filled with children. Mother Teresa was too busy to worry about where the money would come from to pay for the home. She had faith that God would provide.

Missionaries of Charity sisters cared for the children and provided the older ones with an education. Sometimes, the children who had been sick and were now healthy could return to live with their families. The sisters sought families who would adopt the orphans or sponsors who would help pay for the expenses of caring for them. All across Calcutta,

Giving with Little to Give

Many people donated to Mother Teresa's charity, but the ones who had the least to give impressed her the most. She told a story about a four-year-old boy who had heard that Mother Teresa had no sugar for the children in her care. He told his parents that for three days, instead of eating sugar, he would give the sugar to Mother Teresa. His parents brought the sugar in a little bottle to the children's home run by Mother Teresa's Missionaries of Charity. "He could scarcely pronounce my name," she said, "but yet he gave and the love he put in the giving was beautiful."[11]

Mother Teresa's good works spread to more and more of those in need—from the newborns brought to the doors of Shishu Bhavan to the elderly in Nirmal Hriday. ⌒

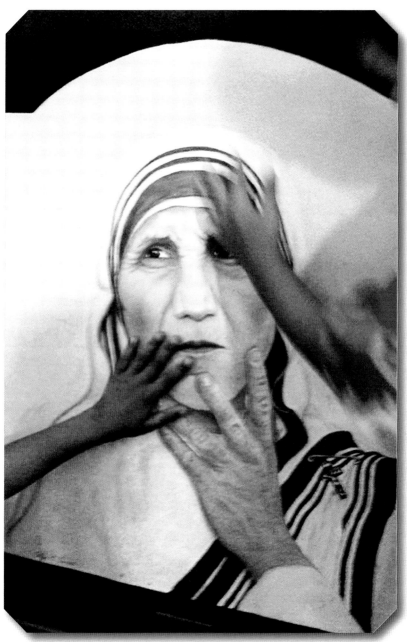

Children in the Shishu Bhavan orphanage touched an image of
Mother Teresa a few days after her death in 1997.

A Calcutta slum in the 1950s

REACHING OUT

wo million people lived in the slums of
Calcutta during the 1950s. There was great
need for help for these poor people. Mother Teresa's
work had begun with the tiny school in Motijhil,
but soon other schools opened to meet the demand.

Word spread of her work. Not only did more poor people come to receive food, schooling, and medical treatment, but also more teachers, doctors, nurses, and nuns joined in to help with the work. "The poor must know that we love them, that they are wanted. They themselves have nothing to give but love," said Mother Teresa. "We are concerned with how to get this message across. We are trying to bring peace to the world through our work. But the work is the gift of God."[1]

Mother Teresa knew people all over India needed help. The rules of the Roman Catholic Church had not permitted the expansion of the Missionaries of Charity outside the Calcutta diocese until the order had been in existence for at least ten years. In 1959, when she was permitted to do so, Mother Teresa wasted no time in expanding her first missionary work beyond Calcutta. She opened homes in Ranchi, Delhi, and Bombay. Prime Minister Jawaharlal Nehru was in attendance at the opening of a children's home in Delhi, India's capital. He told Mother Teresa he had come because he wanted to meet this nun whose work for the poor was quickly becoming famous across India.

India's Caste System

India's social system is made up of castes. This division is part of the most ancient form of Hinduism. Hinduism teaches that humans have a duty to perform in society. The word caste refers to the traditional divisions of Indian society. A person is born into a specific caste. There are more than 3,000 castes in the nation, and each caste has its own set of privileges and limitations that are transferred from one generation to the next. Traditionally, there has been widespread discrimination based on caste.

Although India's 1950 constitution outlaws discrimination against lower castes, it still occurs. Members of higher castes could get better jobs and education than those in lower castes. Members of the lowest caste are referred to as "untouchables." These people are shunned. Many lower-caste Hindus converted to Islam or Christianity.

Mother Teresa believed God was working through the Missionaries of Charity sisters to help the poor, the abandoned, and the sick. Her strength to carry on her work came from God. She said, "Very often I feel like a little pencil in God's Hands. He does the writing, He does the thinking, He does the movement, I have only to be the pencil."[2]

Traveling Abroad, Recognition, and Expanding the Missionaries

In 1960, Mother Teresa made her first international trip as the head of the Missionaries of Charity and drew large audiences who came to hear her speak. She visited the United States, Britain, Germany, Switzerland, and Rome. In 1962, her good works were recognized by the Ramon Magsaysay Award Foundation, which gave her an award for international understanding. The award honors service to the peoples of Asia. The same year, the Indian government awarded her the Padma Shri Award for exceptional and distinguished service.

In 1963, Mother Teresa recognized the need to begin a new part of her congregation, one which could better help men and older boys. She found a priest to become the head of the Missionaries of Charity Brothers, a new order doing much the same work as the sisters. Soon, approximately 15 brothers joined and began a ministry to homeless men and orphaned boys who lived in Calcutta's Howrah railway station. The brothers helped train the men and boys for work and provided them with medical care.

The head of the Roman Catholic Church, Pope Paul VI, came to India in 1964 and stopped to pay a visit to Mother Teresa and the sisters during his trip. He brought with him a luxurious white automobile, which had been a gift to him from the University of Notre Dame in Indiana. The pope gave the car to Mother Teresa when he left. As the head of

"There is much suffering in the world—very much. And the material suffering is suffering from hunger, suffering from homelessness, from all kinds of disease, but I still think that the greatest suffering is being lonely, feeling unloved, just having no one. I have come more and more to realize that it is being unwanted that is the worst disease that any human being can ever experience."[3]

—*Mother Teresa*

Mother Teresa visited Pope Paul VI at the Vatican in 1971.

an order pledged to live like and serve the poor, she had no use for such an extravagant car. In an effort to raise money to build a home for lepers, Mother Teresa suggested they sell raffle tickets with the car as the prize. The raffle raised 460,000 Indian rupees, which was equivalent to approximately $100,000. The money was used to build Shanti Nagar, "City of Peace," which was opened on land donated by the Indian government.

A Trial of Faith

While Mother Teresa's fame grew, she experienced a trial of faith, which she revealed to only a few of her closest advisers. She wrote letters that describe how she felt abandoned by God. "The place of God in my soul is blank," she wrote.

> *There is no God in me.—When the pain of longing is so great—I just long & long for God—and then it is that I feel— He does not want me—He is not there.* [4]

Her mind was filled with questions about her relationship with God. During a retreat in the spring of 1959, in response to a set of personal questions, she wrote, "I don't believe I have a soul." [5] However, throughout her life, Mother Teresa considered suffering to be a gift that brought her closer to Jesus, who suffered death on a cross. And suffering also brought her closer to the poor. She eventually came to believe that her trial was a great part of her mission, as it gave her compassion for the ones she served.

These private letters were published in *Come Be My Light*. The book details her trial of faith, which began shortly after she started the Missionaries of Charity and continued throughout her life. She had asked that her writings be destroyed, but not all of them were. The book was compiled by Father Brian Kolodiejchuk of the Missionaries of Charity.

GROWTH OF THE MISSIONARIES OF CHARITY AROUND THE WORLD

In 1965, Pope Paul VI raised the status of Mother Teresa's Missionaries of Charity order in recognition of her success. The order had grown from one nun teaching a handful of slum children to more than 100 sisters. Instead of reporting to the archbishop of Calcutta, Mother Teresa now was under the direction of only the pope. This allowed her to expand her work outside India for the first time. She began by opening a home in Cocorote, Venezuela, where the sisters began their ministry by teaching children and visiting the poor and the sick.

After this first expansion, requests came quickly to open more homes. In 1968, the pope invited Mother Teresa to open a home for the poor in Rome. Requests came from Tanzania in Africa and Jordan in the Middle East. She soon opened homes in Australia, the United Kingdom, and the United States. Mother Teresa was becoming well known around the world as an advocate for the poor.

Mother Teresa held an orphaned baby girl in Calcutta in 1978.

More sisters and brothers joined in the work, and soon there were homes on every continent except Antarctica.

Many people wanted to help Mother Teresa in her work, but not all of them wanted to become nuns or priests. Many people volunteered for a short period of time to work alongside the sisters of the Missionaries of Charity to help the poor. In 1969, Mother Teresa started a group called the Co-Workers of Mother Teresa, a term borrowed from Indian leader Gandhi. The idea was to create an association of people of any religion and from many countries who would unite in prayer and sacrifice for the goal of service to the poor.

Even though many people worked for the Missionaries of Charity around the world, Mother Teresa knew her work impacted only a tiny portion of the people who needed help. She wanted to make sure all forms of poverty were treated, not just the kind of poverty that causes hunger. She wanted to help people who were lonely or spiritually poor. She began working to open homes in the more developed Western world. The Missionaries of Charity began ministries to help the elderly in Western cities, where the elderly had little interaction with people. Mother Teresa also opened homes in countries she felt needed spiritual guidance, such as Russia and Albania, where churches were closed during Communist rule.

Mother Teresa directed her Co-Workers to focus on doing small, kind things, such as helping a blind man write a letter or picking someone a flower. "Never let anyone come to you without coming away better and happier," she said. "Everyone should see goodness in your face, in your eyes, in your smile."[6]

In the Spotlight

Mother Teresa was interviewed on British television in 1968. The response to the broadcast was overwhelming. Many people encouraged her by sending her money to fund her work. Mother Teresa's fame and influence were growing.

In 1975, Mother Teresa appeared on the cover of the weekly news magazine *Time*, along with a headline, "Living Saints." Her dedication to the poor and words of wisdom brought her respect, fame, and awards. She was awarded the Pope John XXIII Peace Prize in 1971 by the pope. Later

Winning the Nobel Peace Prize

The Nobel Peace Prize is regarded as one of the highest honors in the world. It has been awarded to presidents and political leaders as well as to organizations aimed at making the world a safer place. Winners over the years include: American civil rights champion Martin Luther King Jr. (1964), the International Committee of the Red Cross (1917, 1944, and 1963), and South African presidents Nelson Mandela and F. W. de Klerk (1993).

When Mother Teresa was awarded the Nobel Peace Prize, she asked those present to recite aloud one of her favorite prayers: the prayer of St. Francis of Assisi. It reads:

Lord, make me an instrument of your peace; where there is hatred, let me sow love; where there is injury, pardon; where there is doubt, faith; where there is despair, hope; where there is darkness, light; and where there is sadness, joy; Grant that I may not so much seek to be consoled as to console; to be understood, as to understand, to be loved as to love; for it is in giving that we receive, it is in pardoning that we are pardoned, and it is in dying that we are born to eternal life. Amen.[7]

the same year, she won an award from the Joseph P. Kennedy Jr. Foundation. In 1972, she received the Nehru Award for international understanding. The following year, she received the Templeton Prize for Progress in Religion. In 1978, she was awarded the Balzan Prize for Humanity, Peace and Brotherhood among Peoples. The most important award of all came in 1979 when Mother Teresa was awarded the prestigious Nobel Peace Prize. If she did not have the world's attention before, she had it now.

Mother Teresa accepted the Nobel Peace Prize and other awards that came her way by deflecting the attention toward God and the poor. "I am unworthy," she said, "but thank God for this blessed gift for the poor."[8] She used the money that often came along with awards to help fund her projects. The Magsaysay and Kennedy awards helped build children's homes. The Pope's Peace Prize award money and the Nobel Peace Prize funds were directed toward homes and treatment for lepers. The Nobel Peace Prize brought her not only money and a plaque, but it also focused the world's attention on this elderly Catholic nun who had labored for 30 years on behalf of the poor.

Men and women photographed Mother Teresa as
she arrived in the Vatican in 1980.

*Mother Teresa reacted to winning the Nobel Peace Prize as
she read the announcement in a news dispatch.*

RECOGNITION

fter Mother Teresa was awarded the
Nobel Peace Prize, she became a
reluctant celebrity. Presidents and princes wanted
to be photographed with her. She was awarded
honorary degrees by prestigious universities.

India gave her its top award, the Bharat Ratna, the "Jewel of India." England's Queen Elizabeth presented Mother Teresa with the Honorary Order of Merit. US President Ronald Reagan presented her with the United States' highest civilian honor, the Presidential Medal of Freedom.

PEACEMAKER

All the attention made Mother Teresa uncomfortable, but she understood that she could use it to her advantage: to direct the world's gaze toward issues where she could help people in need. Because she was now regarded as one of the most influential women in the world, Mother Teresa was urged to intervene in international crises. She was asked to lobby for the freedom of 52 US citizens who were held hostage by radical militant students at the US Embassy in Tehran, Iran, from November 1979 to January 1981.

An Added Donation

When Mother Teresa heard there would be a grand and formal banquet following her reception of the Nobel Peace Prize in Oslo, Norway, she requested that it be canceled. She asked that the money saved be added to the award so that more money could go to the service of the poor. Touched by this gesture, children from Norway and other European countries raised money in her honor, which was also donated to the poor.

Mother Teresa spoke with one of the children rescued from West Beirut.

In 1982, Pope John Paul II sent her to Beirut, Lebanon, where a war raged between Israeli and Arab forces. She arrived in Beirut during an intense round of fighting. Snipers were firing shots and bombs fell nearby. She prayed for a cease-fire

so she could make a rescue mission into the war
zone, where a group of mentally and physically
handicapped children were trapped with little food
or water to sustain them. Many of their caregivers
had fled in fear for their lives. The Israeli and
Palestinian fighters gave her the break she needed
to make her rescue mission. She was able to go into
war-torn West Beirut to rescue 37 of the children,
who were huddled together in fear.

HEALTH ISSUES AND A VISIT FROM THE POPE

Even though she was in her seventies, Mother
Teresa still continued her grueling schedule. When
she was at the Mother House in Calcutta, she rose
before dawn for prayer, did chores, attended Mass,
and often worked until very late at night. Overseeing
the Missionaries of Charity homes and the work of
the sisters took her all around the world. In 1983,
while on a visit to Rome, she suffered a major heart
attack. She had emergency surgery there and was
forced to take time off during her recovery. Her
doctors urged her to slow down, and she began
to share her duties with some of the sisters. They
traveled in her place on long journeys to visit the
Missionaries of Charity homes around the world.

In 1986, Pope John Paul II visited Calcutta to see for himself what this amazing nun had created there. He toured Nirmal Hriday, gave his blessings to the residents, and helped feed the people. Mother Teresa called his visit the happiest day of her life.

LEPERS OF THE WEST

Mother Teresa had demonstrated courage many times throughout her life. She did so again in a very public way by visiting patients who were sickened by a new disease that was quickly spreading around the world in the 1980s. She visited patients in Washington DC who were afflicted by acquired immunodeficiency syndrome (AIDS). At the time, many of the victims were shunned because it was not well understood how the disease spread and because the majority of those who were ill were gay men or intravenous drug users.

Famine in Ethiopia

A drought and the mishandling of food aid in Ethiopia caused a famine. Approximately 1 million people died in 1984–1985. Mother Teresa helped organize famine relief and oversee the efforts of her Missionaries of Charity, which operated five homes in Ethiopia to feed the poor.

When Mother Teresa visited a San Francisco church in 1986, she urged churchgoers to show care and compassion for AIDS patients.

Mother Teresa saw a parallel between these outcasts and the lepers in India. She gathered resources and began building hospices for AIDS patients in the United States and Europe. At the time, most AIDS patients were concentrated in advanced Western nations. With these hospices, she wanted to give those who were afflicted with AIDS a place where they could live out their dying days being comforted and cared for, just as she had done for the dying lepers in Calcutta at Nirmal Hriday.

It was not always children and the sick who Mother Teresa felt called upon to help. She also continued her ministry to the unwanted and unloved. She spoke against abortion and against the death penalty. Both, she thought, violated the sacredness of human life. In 1987, she made a visit to San Quentin, a high-security prison

Visit to San Quentin Prison

Michael Wayne Hunter, a convicted inmate in California's San Quentin Prison, was waiting for his execution date on death row when Mother Teresa came to visit the prison in 1987. He saw what many people who met her saw: a drop of goodness in a sad and lonely world. One of the condemned men described her as "this tiny woman who looked one hundred years old."[1] Hunter had no reason to be nice to her or show any respect, because his fate was sealed. But in Mother Teresa, he saw goodness. He wrote,

Incredible vitality and warmth came from her wizened, piercing eyes. She smiled at me, blessed a religious medal, and handed it to me. I wouldn't have walked voluntarily to the front of the tier to see the Warden, the Governor, the President, or the Pope. I could not care less about them. But standing before this woman, all I could say was, "Thank you, Mother Teresa." Then I stepped back to let another dead man come forward to receive his medal.[2]

in California where inmates on death row await
execution. She visited the most dangerous prisoners
in the facility and urged them to trust and love Jesus.

BREAKING DOWN BARRIERS

Communist countries officially banned all forms
of religion. It was a difficult battle to convince
authorities to allow a Catholic nun to serve as a
missionary in the Communist bloc of countries
in Eastern Europe, the Union of Soviet Socialist
Republics (USSR), and China. But Mother Teresa
lobbied and managed to win approval to visit China
in 1985. She dreamed of establishing homes for the
people in this densely populated country, but the
authorities responded to her requests by saying that
the Chinese government took care of its own people.
Her attempts to open a home for handicapped
children continued for several years, but she was
never successful in convincing the authorities to
allow her to establish a presence in China.

In 1986, a nuclear power plant in the USSR
malfunctioned and released radiation into the
surrounding area. The Chernobyl nuclear plant
disaster killed approximately 50 people and posed
long-term health risks to hundreds of thousands

of people in the surrounding areas. Mother Teresa went to Chernobyl to advocate for the victims of the radiation poisoning and to convince Soviet officials to allow her to open a home run by the Missionaries of Charity there.

In 1988, a massive earthquake struck Armenia, also part of the USSR, and Mother Teresa again went to the scene of destruction to offer help. She set up an orphanage to care for the children whose parents were among the 55,000 people who had been killed. Her missions quickly spread throughout the countries of the USSR and Eastern Europe once the Berlin Wall came down in 1989. By this time, the Missionaries of Charity operated more than 350 homes in 80 countries and was growing rapidly.

One place she desperately wanted to visit was Albania, the homeland of her parents. Not only was Albania part of the Communist bloc, it had long been ruled by an atheist dictator, who banned all religious activity. Even after the dissolution of the USSR in 1991, Albania still held strong to Communist ideas. Priests and nuns there had spent decades in prisons. Churches were long closed and converted for other uses. Albanians were not permitted to travel, which Mother Teresa had experienced when she unsuccessfully tried to obtain permission for her mother and sister to leave the country to visit her.

Mother Teresa persisted in trying to bring her missionary work to Albania. Eventually, with the increasing freedom spreading throughout the rest of Eastern Europe, the Albanian authorities gave their approval. She and a group of sisters went to Albania in 1989; she was greeted as a native hero. While in Tirana, Albania, Mother Teresa visited the graves of her mother and sister, who had died in the early 1970s. Within five weeks, she had opened three Missionaries of Charity homes in Albania.

Health Issues Return

While experiencing these personal victories, she struggled with health problems. She had surgery in one eye for a cataract, which was blurring

The Leader of an Army

Mother Teresa's brother, Lazar, lived in Italy and had served in the Italian army during World War II. After seeing her again he said, "You could really say that she is the commander of a unit—indeed of a whole army. She has incredible strength of will, as our mother had. She is a conscientious and disciplined Catholic. This discipline is something she has and so has her entire congregation. It is a very austere Order, organized down to the smallest detail, with very precise rules. And she is their leader."[3]

her vision. She also grew increasingly stooped as osteoporosis weakened her spine. In 1989, she was hospitalized for heart problems again and fitted with a pacemaker to control her irregular heartbeat. She was also treated for malaria.

In April 1990, Mother Teresa told Pope John Paul II she needed to resign as the head of the Missionaries of Charity. He reluctantly accepted her decision, realizing it would be in the best interest of her health if she could stop the constant travel and work on behalf of the poor. The sisters of the Missionaries of Charity, on the other hand, were not ready for her to step down. In September, they reelected 80-year-old Mother Teresa as their leader.

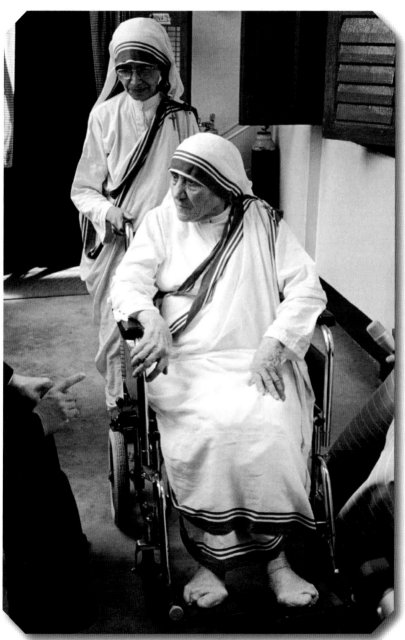

In the 1980s and 1990s, Mother Teresa suffered health issues,
including heart and eye problems.

Nuns from the Missionaries of Charity in Calcutta sang
"Happy Birthday" to Mother Teresa in 1990.

FINAL DAYS AND
BEATIFICATION

Mother Teresa accepted the sisters'
wish that she continue to lead the
Missionaries of Charity, but her declining health
forced her to slow down. Despite her frailty, new
homes continued to open in the early 1990s.

Many were located in the former Communist bloc countries, some were intended for AIDS sufferers in the developed Western world, and more were opened in Africa and South America. She also continued to lobby for peace by writing letters to the leaders of Iraq and the United States when the two countries were at war in 1991.

In 1994, Mother Teresa made another trip to China to convince its authorities to allow the sisters to care for the poor there, but she did not succeed. All the while, she continued receiving more awards. She opened more homes and followed the teachings of the Roman Catholic Church by continuing to speak out against abortion and the death penalty and in favor of natural family planning. Accolades for Mother Teresa and her work continued as well. She was made an honorary US citizen in 1996. A 1999 Gallup/*CNN/USA Today* poll found Mother Teresa to be the most admired person of the century.

CRITICS

Despite her unofficial title as a living saint, there were those who criticized Mother Teresa, the work she was doing, and the way she ran her order. From the very beginning, she welcomed contributions from anyone who gave of their own free will to help the poor. But in the 1990s, she was criticized for taking contributions from people who were wealthy from dishonest means. People such as Haiti's dictator, Jean-Claude Duvalier, and American banker Charles Keating gave her money that may not have been theirs to give because it was obtained in illegal ways. Keating was convicted of swindling investors out of millions of dollars. Some of Keating's victims were poor people who had lost their life savings.

Some nuns, such as Australian Colette Livermore, left the order. Livermore charged that the Missionaries of Charity placed more importance on obedience to the order's rules than on compassionate care of the needy. On several occasions, the needy and the sick were turned away because they showed up at an inconvenient time or place. Livermore said she suggested ways to improve the work of the Missionaries

"The Society demanded that I have no mind of my own and censored everything I read, a form of brainwashing that had almost turned me into an automaton. It asked me to surrender my judgment and the ability to discern. And it told me not to judge another and not to speak or intervene if something cruel or unjust was occurring. It did all this in God's name. He was supposed to be pulling the strings behind the scenes to make everything turn out okay."[1]

—Colette Livermore, part of the Missionaries of Charity, 1973–1984

of Charity and was criticized for questioning authority. For example, she thought improving the diet of the people they worked with in the rural Philippines would strengthen their health. The sisters in charge resisted these ideas and punished her for questioning their authority.

It was also alleged that some of the money donated to the Missionaries of Charity sat in banks for long periods of time instead of going quickly into immediate efforts for disaster relief or general relief for the poor. Another nun who left the order, Susan Shields, said although they received many donations, they were rarely able to spend the money on the poor they were supposed to be helping. Instead, they were told to plead poverty in order to convince more donors to continue giving money.

There were complaints about improper medical training for the sisters and rough handling of children. Tales were told of unhygienic conditions that made those who were treatable sicker than when they had arrived. Simple comfort measures were not taken: pain-relieving drugs were not offered and patients were bathed in cold water. Needles were being reused, which easily passed on diseases. Those who were contagious were not properly separated from the rest of the patient population, posing a danger to healthy nuns and other patients. In her defense, Mother Teresa explained that the medical training the sisters received was limited, but what they provided, in most cases, was assistance the people would not receive from anyone else.

Her critics also pointed out that while the destitute received second-rate care, Mother Teresa was taken to the best modern hospitals and treated by the top doctors when she was ill. Some Indian scholars criticized the fact that her work shone a negative light on their country as one of perpetual poverty. They thought her work portrayed the Indian people as unable to bring themselves out of their squalor without explaining the historical colonization that had led to the conditions.

Some criticized Mother Teresa for focusing on the details rather than the big picture. She was concerned about the individual poor person, but she did not focus her efforts on preventing people from needing her charity's help in the future. The sisters taught natural family planning methods to the people, but these methods were not enough to address the problem of overpopulation in countries such as India.

Mother Teresa never wanted to be seen as a social worker. As she felt the need to explain frequently throughout her life, her work was for Jesus. She said,

All we do—our prayer, our work, our suffering—is for Jesus. Our life has no other reason or motivation. This is a point many people do not understand. I serve Jesus twenty-four hours a day. Whatever I do is for Him. And He gives me the strength. I love Him in the poor and the poor in Him, but always the Lord comes first. [2]

FINAL DAYS

In December 1991, on a trip to visit one of her missions in Tijuana, Mexico, Mother Teresa became ill with bacterial pneumonia. Doctors determined she was suffering from heart failure and needed an angioplasty. She was transferred to a more modern and well-equipped hospital in La Jolla, California.

As Mother Teresa's health declined, she grew more dependent on those around her. When she was hospitalized in Rome in 1992 and in

An Indian Citizen by Choice

After living in India for many years, Mother Teresa became a citizen of India in 1948. Years later, when asked if she considered herself Indian, she described her love for the country. However, she summed up the differences between her and the man who questioned her when she stated, "You are an Indian by accident (of birth); I am an Indian by choice." [3]

Delhi in 1993, many began speculating what would
happen to the Missionaries of Charity without her
leadership. In 1996, she suffered a series of falls,
continued suffering heart problems, and underwent
surgery in November.

Although she was not well, Mother Teresa and
the sisters gathered to commemorate an important
date on September 10, 1996. It was the fiftieth
anniversary of Inspiration Day, the day on the train
to Darjeeling when God called her to go out and
serve the poor. In January 1997, Mother Teresa
announced her intention once again to resign as
head of the Missionaries of Charity. The sisters
elected a new leader on March 13, 1997. Mother
Teresa's successor, Sister Nirmala Joshi, was born
into a Hindu family in India and was inspired by
the work of the Missionaries of Charity to convert to
Catholicism at age 24.

Although her order was in the hands of a new
leader, Mother Teresa was still the symbolic leader
of the Missionaries of Charity. In that role, she went
to Rome on May 16, 1997, to meet with Pope John
Paul II. She also traveled to the United States to meet
with new sisters and to receive the Congressional
Gold Medal.

*People gathered to view Mother Teresa's body
in Calcutta in September 1997.*

Mother Teresa celebrated her eighty-seventh
birthday on August 26, 1997, in Calcutta. A few
days later, on September 5, 1997, she died. Her
heart had given out. The people of India, who
proudly claimed Mother Teresa as their own, went
into a national day of mourning. Tens of thousands
lined the streets of Calcutta to pay their respects as
her body was transported on the same gun carriage
that had carried previous national heroes Gandhi
and Nehru. India honored her with a state funeral
attended by many world leaders.

PATH TO SAINTHOOD

Pope John Paul II wasted little time in beginning the process to have Mother Teresa declared a saint by the Roman Catholic Church. Saints are honored for living a life that is an example of faith and love. In most cases, the person lived an exemplary life, often in service to others. He or she has also been credited with at least two miracles such as healing a person who is sick. The process takes many years and usually begins with a five-year waiting period after a person's death before the individual can be considered.

Catholics often speak of praying to a certain saint for help. Patron saints are believed to help in various areas of life. For example, a person who needs help finding his or her way may say a prayer to Saint Christopher, the patron saint of motorists and travelers.

In Mother Teresa's case, a team was put together to investigate the claims of miracles performed, a requirement for sainthood. Church authorities accepted one claim of a miracle, when a Hindu woman was said to be healed of a cancerous tumor after praying to Mother Teresa and holding a religious medal Mother Teresa had touched against her belly. On October 19, 2003, the pope announced the beatification of Mother Teresa. This is the first step in the path toward sainthood. She is now referred to as Blessed Mother Teresa of Calcutta. Another miracle must be verified by the church before she can be canonized as a saint.

A Life of Service

People who heard about this "Saint of the Gutter" could not help but be impressed by tales of her selflessness. But as she explained it, it was her deep and continuing love of Jesus and dedication to the ideal of serving him in the distressing disguise of the poor that got her through the difficult work she chose. "It is not how much we give—but how much love we put in the giving," she explained.[4]

After her private letters were published in 2007, it became known that she did not feel like God was speaking to her or listening to her prayers during most of her later years. Still, she persisted in the work.

Mother Teresa's Resting Place

The move by the Roman Catholic Church to fast-track Mother Teresa's elevation to sainthood has created a new controversy. Albanians claim her as their own and are demanding the return of her remains. Although Mother Teresa acknowledged her Albanian heritage, she always emphasized that she was a citizen of India. This shows that many loved her, but that the strife between peoples and nations she worked so tirelessly to overcome still remains.

Her example of selflessly giving
up all material comforts to seek
a spiritual life of service inspired
others to follow in her footsteps.
As of September 2010, there were
more than 5,000 sisters serving in
765 houses in 137 countries—520 of
these houses in countries other than
India. The Missionaries of Charity
Brothers continue to flourish, and
there are also many thousands of
volunteers.

For people throughout the world,
Mother Teresa led by example. She
put her own comforts aside to help
and live like those who had been
ignored by the rest of the world. This
tiny woman became a familiar face
to millions. She inspired thousands
of people with her extraordinary
dedication and simple words. She
said, "The poor do not need our
compassion or our pity; they need
our help."[5]

A Simple Life

Mother Teresa was entombed in the Mother House in Calcutta under a plain stone slab. Mass is said daily at the site, which has been converted to a chapel. The simple room where she lived has been kept as it was when she died. It contains a cot with a thin mattress, a writing desk, a chair, a table, and two stools. A picture of Jesus with a crown of thorns hangs on the wall. Close by, a small museum displays some of Mother Teresa's personal items, such as her sari and sandals.

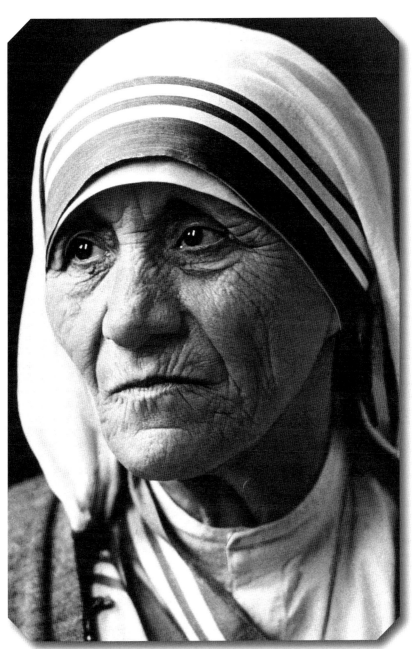

*Mother Teresa's influence continues through her organizations
dedicated to serving the poor.*

TIMELINE

1910	1928	1929
Agnes Gonxha Bojaxhiu is born in Skopje, Ottoman Empire, on August 26.	On September 26, Agnes leaves home to enter the Sisters of Loreto Order and begin her training in Ireland.	On January 6, Agnes, now Sister Teresa, arrives in Calcutta, India, for the first time.

1946	1946	1947
The Muslim League declares Direct Action Day on August 16. A week of street fighting follows.	On September 10, Mother Teresa hears God give her the call within a call while on a train to Darjeeling.	India becomes a nation on August 15. The British divide the colony into two independent countries: India and Pakistan.

1931

Sister Teresa takes her first vows as a nun in Darjeeling, India, on May 24. She begins teaching in Entally, Calcutta.

1937

Sister Teresa takes her final vows at the convent in Darjeeling in May.

1937

Sister Teresa is made headmistress of St. Mary's school. From this time on, she is known as Mother Teresa.

1948

Mother Teresa becomes a citizen of India.

1948

Mother Teresa begins working with and living as the poorest of the poor in Calcutta in August.

1950

The Missionaries of Charity congregation officially begins on October 7.

TIMELINE

1952

On August 22, Nirmal Hriday opens near the Kali Temple in Calcutta to serve the dying destitute.

1955

Shishu Bhavan, the first Missionaries of Charity children's home, opens in Calcutta on September 23.

1962

Mother Teresa wins her first major international awards, the Magsaysay Award and the Padma Shri Award.

1982

On August 14, Mother Teresa rescues handicapped children who had been trapped in a war zone in Beirut, Lebanon.

1989

Mother Teresa visits her ancestral homeland of Albania.

1990

After suffering health problems, Mother Teresa resigns as head of the Missionaries of Charity, but the sisters reelect her as their leader.

1964

Pope Paul VI visits India and gives Mother Teresa his car, which she raffles off to raise money to build Shanti Nagar, a home for lepers.

1965

Pope Paul VI raises the status of the Missionaries of Charity, allowing the order to establish homes outside India for the first time.

1979

Mother Teresa is announced as the winner of the Nobel Peace Prize.

1997

Mother Teresa again resigns as head of the Missionaries of Charity in January.

1997

Mother Teresa dies on September 5 at the Mother House in Calcutta.

2003

Mother Teresa is beatified by Pope John Paul II on October 19 in front of thousands at the Vatican.

Essential Facts

Date of Birth

August 26, 1910 (born Agnes Gonxha Bojaxhiu)

Place of Birth

Skopje, Ottoman Empire (Skopje is now the capital of Macedonia, which became independent in 1912.)

Date of Death

September 5, 1997

Parents

Nikola and Dranafile (Drana) Bojaxhiu

Education

Agnes attended the Sacred Heart Church school. She received training to become a Catholic nun at Rathfarnham, near Dublin, Ireland. She completed her initial novitiate training at Darjeeling, India.

Marriage

None.

Children

None.

CAREER HIGHLIGHTS

Sister Teresa taught at the St. Mary's school in Calcutta for 17 years. As Mother Teresa, she began her own order, the Missionaries of Charity, to serve the people living in the slums of Calcutta. Mother Teresa received many awards for her charitable work, none more prestigious than the Nobel Peace Prize in 1979. She became known as a living saint, expanding her work to every continent except Antarctica.

SOCIETAL CONTRIBUTION

Mother Teresa opened homes for the dying, orphaned children, and lepers. She served the poorest of the poor in India and around the world.

CONFLICTS

While her missions around the world continued to expand, Mother Teresa's personal and spiritual life were often difficult. She had many health problems and sometimes felt that God had abandoned her.

QUOTE

"Never let anyone come to you without coming away better and happier. Everyone should see goodness in your face, in your eyes, in your smile." —*Mother Teresa*

Glossary

abortion
The intentional ending of a pregnancy.

AIDS
Acquired Immunodeficiency Syndrome; a serious viral disease that attacks the body's immune system and often leads to death.

angioplasty
The surgical repair of a blood vessel.

baptism
A Christian ceremony in which a person is immersed or sprinkled with water and admitted into the Christian community.

beatification
The official act of the pope whereby a deceased person is declared to be worthy of receiving religious honor.

canonization
The process through which a person is declared an official saint.

communism
A system in which society shares the means of production, goods are distributed to all, and social classes do not exist.

diocese
The jurisdiction of a bishop in the Catholic Church.

hospice
A home or facility that provides care to people who are terminally ill.

malaria
A disease characterized by chills and fever; the disease is spread by mosquitoes.

missionary
A person who travels to another country or region with the intention of preaching religious beliefs and serving the native population.

novice
> A person who is training to be a nun.

nun
> A member of a female religious group who has usually taken vows.

order
> A group of people who live together under a common religious belief and live by a set of rules or doctrine.

partition
> The dividing of an area into separate countries, each with its own government.

pilgrimage
> A religious journey taken to pay respect to a sacred place.

postulant
> A person who applies to a religious order as a candidate for membership.

rupee
> The currency of India.

saint
> A person officially recognized by the Roman Catholic Church as one who is holy; a saint must go through a process of canonization.

sari
> A traditional South Asian dress made of a long piece of cloth wrapped around the body to form a skirt and top.

slum
> A poor and crowded area.

tuberculosis
> An infectious disease that attacks the lungs and other parts of the body.

vocation
> An area of work.

ADDITIONAL RESOURCES

SELECTED BIBLIOGRAPHY

Chawla, Navin. *Mother Teresa: The Authorized Biography*. Rockport, MA: Element, 1997. Print.

Collopy, Michael. *Works of Love are Works of Peace*. San Francisco: Ignatius Press, 1996. Print.

Gonzalez-Balado, Jose Luis, and Janet N. Playfoot, eds. *My Life for the Poor: Mother Teresa of Calcutta*. San Francisco: Harper & Row, 1985. Print.

Porter, David. *Mother Teresa: The Early Years*. Grand Rapids, MI: Eerdman's, 1986. Print.

Spink, Kathryn. *Mother Teresa: A Complete Authorized Biography*. San Francisco: HarperSanFrancisco, 1997. Print.

FURTHER READINGS

Gold, Maya. *Mother Teresa*. New York: DK Publishing, 2008. Print.

Scott, David. *A Revolution of Love: The Meaning of Mother Teresa*. Chicago: Loyola Press, 2005. Print.

Slavicek, Louise Shipley. *Mother Teresa: Caring for the World's Poor*. New York: Chelsea House, 2007. Print.

Web Links

To learn more about Mother Teresa, visit ABDO Publishing Company online at **www.abdopublishing.com**. Web sites about Mother Teresa are featured on our Book Links page. These links are routinely monitored and updated to provide the most current information available.

Places to Visit

Basilica of the National Shrine of Mary, Queen of the Universe

8300 Vineland Avenue, Orlando, FL 32821
407-239-6600
www.maryqueenoftheuniverse.org
Visit the Shrine of Mary to learn more about the Catholic faith and its history. The Shrine features stained glass, paintings, and sculptures. Visitors can attend Mass and visit the outdoor chapel.

United States Institute of Peace

1200 Seventeenth Street NW, Washington, DC 20036
202-457-1700
www.usip.org
The United States Institute of Peace provides training to promote building peace. The institute offers courses to promote stability and end violent international conflicts. It also houses a research library.

SOURCE NOTES

Chapter 1. A Leap of Faith

1. Mother Teresa, and Brian Kolodiejchuk, ed. *Mother Teresa: Come Be My Light, The Private Writings of the "Saint of Calcutta."* New York: Doubleday, 2007. Print. 37.

2. Eileen Egan. *Such a Vision of the Street.* Garden City, NY: Image Books, 1986. Print. 25.

3. Navin Chawla. *Mother Teresa: The Authorized Biography.* Rockport, MA: Element, 1997. Print. 20.

Chapter 2. Growing Up

1. Jose Luis Gonzalez-Balado, and Janet N. Playfoot, eds. *My Life for the Poor: Mother Teresa of Calcutta.* San Francisco: Harper & Row, 1985. Print. 2.

2. Navin Chawla. *Mother Teresa: The Authorized Biography.* Rockport, MA: Element, 1997. Print. 5.

Chapter 3. Entering Religious Life

1. Kathryn Spink. *Mother Teresa: A Complete Authorized Biography.* San Francisco: HarperSanFrancisco, 1997. Print. 13–14.

Chapter 4. Early Years as a Nun

1. David Porter. *Mother Teresa: The Early Years.* Grand Rapids, MI: Eerdman's, 1986. Print. 38.

2. Ibid. 41–42.

3. Edward LeJoly. *We Do It For Jesus: Mother Teresa and her Missionaries of Charity.* Oxford, England: Oxford University Press, 1977. Print. 17.

4. David Porter. *Mother Teresa: The Early Years.* Grand Rapids, MI: Eerdman's, 1986. Print. 47.

5. David Scott. *A Revolution of Love: The Meaning of Mother Teresa.* Chicago: Loyola Press, 2005. Print. 72–73.

Chapter 5. Troubles in India

1. Anne Sebba. *Mother Teresa: Beyond the Image*. New York: Doubleday, 1997. Print. 47.

2. David Porter. *Mother Teresa: The Early Years*. Grand Rapids, MI: Eerdman's, 1986. Print. 61.

Chapter 6. Ministry to the Poor

1. David Porter. *Mother Teresa: The Early Years*. Grand Rapids, MI: Eerdman's, 1986. Print. 75–76.

2. Joanna Hurley. *Mother Teresa: A Pictorial Biography*. Philadelphia: Courage Books, 1997. Print. 64.

3. Navin Chawla. *Mother Teresa: The Authorized Biography*. Rockport, MA: Element, 1997. Print. 74.

4. Ibid. 62.

5. Michael Collopy. *Works of Love are Works of Peace*. San Francisco: Ignatius Press, 1996. Print. 35.

6. Navin Chawla. *Mother Teresa: The Authorized Biography*. Rockport, MA: Element, 1997. Print. 159.

7. Malcolm Muggeridge. *Something Beautiful for God*. San Francisco: Harper & Row, 1971. Print. 119.

8. Kathryn Spink. *Mother Teresa: A Complete Authorized Biography*. San Francisco: HarperSanFrancisco, 1997. Print. 298.

9. Ibid. 56.

10. Navin Chawla. *Mother Teresa: The Authorized Biography*. Rockport, MA: Element, 1997. Print. 161.

11. Jose Luis Gonzalez-Balado, and Janet N. Playfoot, eds. *My Life for the Poor: Mother Teresa of Calcutta*. San Francisco: Harper & Row, 1985. Print. 79.

Source Notes Continued

Chapter 7. Reaching Out

1. Michael Collopy. *Works of Love are Works of Peace*. San Francisco: Ignatius Press, 1996. Print. 72.

2. Mother Teresa, and Brian Kolodiejchuk, ed. *Mother Teresa: Come Be My Light, The Private Writings of the "Saint of Calcutta."* New York: Doubleday, 2007. Print. 363.

3. Michael Collopy. *Works of Love are Works of Peace*. San Francisco: Ignatius Press, 1996. Print. 145.

4. Mother Teresa, and Brian Kolodiejchuk, ed. *Mother Teresa: Come Be My Light, The Private Writings of the "Saint of Calcutta."* New York: Doubleday, 2007. Print. 2.

5. Ibid. 349.

6. Michael Collopy. *Works of Love are Works of Peace*. San Francisco: Ignatius Press, 1996. Print. 178.

7. "Peace Prayer of St. Francis." *AmericanCatholic.org*. Franciscan Friars and St. Anthony Messenger Press, n.d. Web. 6 July 2010.

8. Kathryn Spink. *Mother Teresa: A Complete Authorized Biography.* San Francisco: HarperSanFrancisco, 1997. Print. 167.

Chapter 8. Recognition

1. Joanna Hurley. *Mother Teresa: A Pictorial Biography*. Philadelphia: Courage Books, 1997. Print. 106.

2. Ibid.

3. David Porter. *Mother Teresa: The Early Years.* Grand Rapids, MI: Eerdman's, 1986. Print. 42.

Chapter 9. Final Days and Beatification

1. Colette Livermore. *Hope Endures: Leaving Mother Teresa, Losing Faith and Searching for Meaning.* New York: Free Press, 2008. Print. 179–80.

2. Michael Collopy. *Works of Love are Works of Peace*. San Francisco: Ignatius Press, 1996. Print. 98.

3. Edward LeJoly, and Jaya Chalila, eds. *Mother Teresa's Reaching Out in Love*. New York: Barnes&Noble Books, 1998. Print. 55.

4. Susan Conroy. *Mother Teresa's Lessons of Love & Secrets of Sanctity*. Huntington, IN: Our Sunday Visitor, 2003. Print. 86.

5. Mother Teresa. *No Greater Love.* Novato, CA: New World Library, 1997. Print. 102.

Index

ABOUT THE AUTHOR

Christie Ritter is a journalist and author who has researched and written about government, education, science, nature, health, and business for newspapers, magazines, and Web sites. Her writing awards include First Place recognition in the Environment/ Agriculture, Features, and Science/Health categories from the Society of Professional Journalists. She is a graduate of UCLA, with a Bachelor of Arts in Political Science, and San Diego State University, with a Master of Science in Mass Communications. She is the proud mother of two children. This book is dedicated to them.

PHOTO CREDITS